Sign and Symbol of the Invisible God

SIGN AND SYMBOL
OF THE INVISIBLE GOD

ESSAYS ON THE SACRAMENTS TODAY

Peter J. Riga

FIDES PUBLISHERS, INC.
NOTRE DAME, INDIANA

© COPYRIGHT: 1971, FIDES PUBLISHERS, INC.
NOTRE DAME, INDIANA

NIHIL OBSTAT: BRIAN T. JOYCE
CENSOR LIBRORUM

IMPRIMATUR: FLOYD L. BEGIN, D.D.
BISHOP OF OAKLAND
Feb. 3, 1971

LCCCN: 72-166155
ISBN: 0-8190-0495-2

Contents

Introduction

Catholics today are confused about many things, not least about the changes in "doctrine" and about the things that theologians taught them were unchangeable in the past.

It seems that everything has changed and that the stable rock of doctrine is slowly being eroded, not so much from without but, more insidiously, from within. This, of course, has given rise to a sense of anguish and loneliness on the part of many within the Church.

In a sense, however, this sense of anguish and groping is not all bad. It can be positively good if it will move us out of concepts, formulations and modes of thinking which no longer mean anything to us today. Every thought process is directly dependent upon a human and therefore cultural experience of life as it is lived in each generation. This cannot be dispensed with by appealing to a cultural experience of a (or any) generation of the past (or future). God reveals himself in the only way we can understand him, that is, in the human experience of the present. We have a right and indeed an obligation to compare this experience of faith today (under the guidance of the selfsame Spirit in the Church) with that of former ages, but this latter aspect cannot exempt us from ever starting anew this understanding of faith within the context of our ever new human experience. To do so would be an escape from the reality which we know.

It is precisely this function which belongs to the whole Church but in a particular way to the Catholic theologian. It is he who must consider as his primary duty to translate the truth of faith correctly in the light of human experience today so as to arrive at an ever increasing knowledge and realization of divine faith, ever old and ever new. For faith is not primarily and above all an uttering of truths given once and for all in divine revelation but rather the revealing and living of the person of God to men of each age until ages are no more and "Christ is all things in all things." There is only one truth and he is God, for every age, race and culture. But men come to realize him (insofar as they are concerned) within an understanding of a culture which exists now, not in the past. Therefore, the whole Church, but more particularly the Catholic theologian, must continuously search for the nameless mystery who is God, in every age and in every culture.

Therefore, as we have said, a certain anguish and searching for this reality is not bad. But it can become bad if we panic before the new and the changing in our culture and therefore *of our idea of God*. In reality it is not our faith which changes (this is impossible, for the object of our faith always remains God) but our experience and formulation of this notion of God which is continuously changing.

It has been said with a certain amount of truth that every true Christian must be an atheist. That is, he must recognize that every name and every truth predicated of God, contains some truth but never the whole truth, about God. We must always break out of our idolatrous naming of God, and ever anew go further and deeper into this nameless mystery of our existence. This journey will always be one of trust in the grace of God who calls us ever new to himself in each culture and time and to fear to venture forth, like Abraham, into a dark and unfamiliar place, is to, in reality, not to believe in God at all but rather in our little idea of God (which is not God!). "Go from your country and your kindred and your father's house to the land that I will show you" (Gen 12:1). It was the same then as it is now. We must go forward to an unfamiliar land precisely because the God whom we seek is always beyond our grasp; but we are required to try to understand and, as Vatican I said, with humility we can arrive at least at some knowledge of God.

It was in this spirit that the following work was written. God appears in each age always as sign and symbol, starting with the primordial sign of God's salvation in history, the Incarnation of the Son of God. The Incarnate Word is the efficacious sign that men can see that God has so loved the world that he gave his own beloved Son for its salvation (Jn 3:18).

In the act of this supreme salvific will of God in Christ was born the Church, the presence in history of God's redemptive action in Christ and his body. It is also for this reason that we can also call the Church the primordial and fundamental sacrament of God in the world since the Church is an efficacious sign and extension of Christ's actualized redemption in the world for every age, race, nation, color and time. The Church is truly the *Catholica*.

All of this is fundamental to Christian faith and cannot change as to substance. This actualizing of Christ's redemption appearing in tangible and efficaciously symbolical form is what we call a sacrament. In other words, when the Church as source of redemptive grace officially and publicly meets the individual in the accomplishment of her nature there we have a sacrament. Why? Because the Church is the very actualization or accomplishment of redemptive grace for all men, historically visible and sign of God's very victory in the world.

It is in this sense that we can speak of the seven more particular sacraments in which the Church officially and authoritatively meets man. In supreme moments of his human existence (birth, eating, sexual love and reproduction, entrance into the world, sickness and death and sin), God in the Church confronts him with the efficacious symbols of redemptive grace (baptism, Eucharist, marriage, confirmation, anointing of the sick, penance). Each of these symbols, however, must be understood within the context of human existence today. The substance of the sacrament, as the Council of Trent taught, remains always the same but they become real for us when we can relate this "substance" to the reality of human existence as it exists today.

This is what the following chapters on the sacraments try to do. I have purposely omitted scholarly footnotes, detailed bibliography, etc., for the simple reason that the book is destined for the average reader and should be able to be understood as read in the text. At the end of each chapter, there is a short bibliography for those who wish to pursue the study further.

St. Mary's College   Peter J. Riga
December 1, 1970

CHAPTER I

History of Sacrament

In Vatican II's definition, the Church is called "the sacrament of the intimate union with God and the unity of the human race." (*Constitution on the Church*, par. 1). For our present purposes, we shall leave aside until the next chapter the theological meaning of this statement. We wish here to give a cursory glance at the way in which the word "sacrament" has come down historically to us today.

One of the most popular titles of the Church given to us by Vatican II has been that of the Church as a "sacrament."

> By her relationship with Christ, the Church is a kind of sacrament or sign of intimate union with God, and of the unity of all mankind. (Par. 1)

The term goes back to the Fathers of the Church themselves. The Church likens herself to a sacrament, both as a sign and as instrument. She is a sign, for men who are corporal by nature see the visible Church which bears a divine power toward a spiritual union. An instrument is a means by which an act is accomplished. Thus sacrament was used at Vatican II here in a broad sense, not in the usual sense of particular signs of grace instituted by Christ, the sense we associate with the seven sacraments.

Thus the word "sacrament" holds a central place in the work of Vatican II and as such is one of its master ideas in its description of the Church. The idea of sacrament has at least this over the former juridical idea of the Church: it stresses the complete dependence of the Church upon Christ, as it relates the Church to the same incarnational manifestation in the same economy of salvation as the Word Incarnate.

It is this sacramental consciousness of the Church as a personal community which the early Church had of itself which was expressed above all in the Eucharist.

The union of brothers which is the Church is the fruit of one and the same Spirit who communicates himself to men and becomes in a sense their life-sustaining principle in the body of the Church. Thus, according to St. Cyprian, the unity of the Church, its peace and fraternal union, are gifts of God and a participation in the divine unity of the Father, Son and Holy Spirit. The Church appears as "a people which draws its unity from the Father, Son and Holy Spirit," (*The Lord's Prayer*, 23). This union of men with God and hence, with members of the Church with each other, is a terrestrial and visible reality here below; it is also a divine reality as well which is at once eternal and spiritual. The Church is the religious peace and fraternal union with God inspired by the Holy Spirit as well as life in the alliance (St. Augustine).

From the second century, Latin Christianity employed the term *"sacramentum"* in order to translate the Greek term *"mysterion"* taken by Christians from the Greek translation of the Old Testament (LXX) where it signified a secret deliberation. In the religious domain, *"mysterion"* signified the creating design of God as he reveals it to those who believe in him (Ws 2:22). The manifestation of this mystery is the sign of God's love for men. It separates believers and nonbelievers as it was used clearly in Mt 13:11; Mk 4:11; Lk 8:10. Here, the disciples have access to the mystery of the kingdom of God but it is not given to those who do not believe. The revelation of the mystery in the New Testament signifies that the person who receives it takes part in an intimate relationship with God in the new alliance. For those who believe, the power of God is affirmed and realized in his revelation of mercy and love. There is a second element which is essential for understanding the notion of *mysterion*. In biblical thought, the word of God is always action. Thus, revelation of God's saving design is also its realization. This loving revelation makes the alliance and creates the union between God and the elect. Thus, *"mysterion"* (sacrament) means the salvific plan which God reveals by realizing it in the faithful who believe.

The word has this meaning in the epistles of St. Paul. The eternal design of God is now manifested by the Holy Spirit to those who believe, while it remains incomprehensible to the man of natural reason (1 Cor 2:14). The contents of the mystery is the whole of the gospel or particular aspects of this message such as the resurrection of the dead (1 Cor 15:51) or the same salvation given both to Jew and Gentile alike (Rom 11:25). The gospel is nothing else than Jesus Christ which St. Paul preaches (1 Cor 1:23). Jesus Christ is the true mystery of God. In fact, he is the substance of the eternal and divine design as well as its realization. Thus the *mysterion* is the gospel (Eph 6:19) or Jesus Christ himself (Col 2:2; 4:3; Eph 3:3). The eternal design of God is revealed and is realized by the gospel which is announced to both pagans and Jews (Tit 2:11; 3:4). In dying for our sins and rising by our justification (Gal 4:4; Rom 4:25), in giving us his spirit, Jesus Christ realizes the mystery of God and reveals it to us (1 Tim 3:16). Jesus is thus completely identified with the mystery and is the visible "sacrament" among men.

This identification of the mystery of God and the person of Jesus Christ is important for another reason. From the moment when Jesus Christ is called "the mystery of God," the essential point now is the realization of God's saving design in time and the form in which it becomes accessible to men. From this moment on, the word "mystery" means those events by which the saving design of God is manifested in a veiled way while it realizes itself, that is, the Incarnation itself. In this sense, Jesus is the fundamental sacrament of God's love among men.

In the postapostolic period, there is a further development of this word. Ignatius of Antioch and St. Justin both use the word *mysterion* not only to designate the entire person and work of Jesus, but also the principle events of his life: his virginal birth, his cross and resurrection. Since this period, Christianity spoke of the "mysteries of the life of Jesus," the earthly and human events by which the divine plan is revealed to men by entering the course of time.

Thus, toward the year 200, *mysterion* signified either the eternal and divine plan, powerfully realized and manifested in the person of Jesus Christ who came to save men; or Jesus himself as the revelation and realization in time of the eternal and salvific plan of God.

Such was the Christian notion of *mysterion* in the early Church. The Greek word was translated by the Latin *sacramentum*. It soon became a popular term for the Christian rite of baptism and of the Eucharist—rapidly in the Western Church, more slowly in the East. The development is not altogether clear but very complex. In the fourth and fifth centuries—when the Christian liturgy took its definitive formulation—it became the technical word for the celebration of baptism and the Eucharist. *Sacramentum* was employed to designate the sacrament of initiation into the Christian rites, which therefore never lost its original sense of "initiation."

Thus, the semantic evolution of the term shows that in Christian thought, baptism and the Eucharist naturally had a preeminent place in the effective realization of revelation which was designated as *mysterion-sacramentum*. Soon other rites were added (such as that of the "imposition of hands") since there appeared a certain consciousness of the analogy which related baptism and other rites to the celebration of the Eucharist.

From the beginning, baptism was not only considered to be an incorporation into the new messianic people of God, but also as the pardon of sins and a regeneration, that is, a gift of the Holy Spirit as well as the salvific and living action of God. The baptism of John the Baptist was considered to be an anticipation of the descending of the Spirit in Jesus who died and rose. Thus in the Epistle to the Romans (6:2–5) there was a relationship established between the baptism of the Christian and the death and resurrection of the Lord. In the

epistle to the Colossians (2:11–13) the relationship
of death is implicit but explicit in the resurrection.
The texts we have teach us that this participation
in the death and resurrection of Jesus was not well
developed before 200 but that after that time it
was one of the principle subjects of the doctrine of
baptism. These early Christians saw in baptism a
sort of anticipation of our own resurrection to
come, already realized in a mysterious way in
Jesus (Eph 2:5–6). Thus baptism was a celebration
of the ecclesial community and action of God, relating first of all to the death and resurrection of
Jesus as well as to an eschatological promise for
the future.

A consideration of the Eucharist leads to the
same conclusion. The Eucharist being the sacred
banquet of the community was celebrated from
the beginning as the memorial of the Last Supper.
By it, the faithful were joined to the glorified Lord
and had the privilege of feasting on him who died
and rose for them; Christians thereby participated
in the life and spirit of Jesus. It was very soon considered a foretaste of the heavenly banquet (Lk
22:15–20) and a token of salvation. The *arrhes*
(beginning or foretaste) of the new and eternal life
(Jn 6:32; 53–58). Here we also have an ecclesial
celebration where the Lord nourishes the faithful
who commemorate his death and resurrection,
thereby awaiting its celestial consummation.

Thus both in baptism and in the Eucharist there

was also a certain polarity between the terrestrial action and the salvific action of God, between the concrete word pronounced on the offering of bread and the Spirit with his creating and vivifying power. There was also a singular temporal polarity which related the celebration here and now to a former historical event, that is, to the mystery of the redemption by Jesus Christ and which, in its turn, projected Christians toward the future as its supreme consummation. Thus, towards the year 200 there developed a sacramental conception which, without being uniform, embraced the entire Christian history of salvation realized on earth. This mystery is acting among us and for us. Faith gives us the means to see it, to recognize its meaning and to give our assent to it by abandoning ourselves to it and making it our own, here and now. The work of the primitive Church was to understand that even here below in time, God establishes the alliance of the Incarnation—a full communion with men who are both body and spirit, persons and social beings, present, past and future.

READINGS

1. B. Leeming, *Principles of Sacramental Theology,* (Westminster, Md., 1960).
2. G. McCauley, *Sacraments for Secular Man* (New York, 1969).

3. M. M. Ponty, *Signs* (Northwestern University Press, 1964).

4. *The Sacraments in General: New Perspectives*, (New York, 1967: Concilium Series, vol. 31).

DISCUSSION QUESTIONS

1. What was the original meaning of "sacrament"?
2. What do we mean when we say that Christ is the "sacrament of God"?
3. How is the Church a sacrament?
4. How do the sacraments become real for us today?
5. What makes us one in the Church?
6. What does St. Paul mean when he says that Christ is the mystery of God?

CHAPTER II

Theology of Sacrament

I

We must first understand in what sense Jesus Christ, and after him the Church, can be called the primordial sacraments. *The* sacrament is the eternal and salvific plan of God which is manifested to men by his powerful action. It is the work of God in history since it designates the divine initiative and his action as well as its realization among men. God reveals and realizes his salvific design here below in order that men might recognize him in his hidden manifestation. Men thus can enter into personal relationship with him and find in him their salvation and their happiness. It is an efficacious sign since it expresses the irresistible power of God who calls men to be converted to him.

This essential sacrament is therefore the person of Jesus Christ; in the intervening period between his ascension and his final return (*Parousia*), his body, the Church, represents him. Jesus is the sacramental source. Since the time of the earliest tradition, this reality of Christ's body was the foundation of all Christian sacramentality. Saint Augustine says it well: *"non est aliud mysterium Dei nisi Christus,"* (*Epistle* 187, 11). Christ is such because of his quality of God-man, but more particularly because he is the perfect man, the model type of all and because he represents as man the pure affirmation of the "yes" to the Father. As man, Jesus is obedient because, being the Word consubstantial with the Father, he is the Son eternally generated, perfect reflection of the Father. The mutual relationship consists in his receiving all from the Father, and becoming incarnate for the love of men and obedient to his Father's will. That is why Jesus has perfect liberty with the Father, fully confident of being always heard since a perfect union always exists between them. Thus here below, the perfect union of man and God is accomplished in the person of the new Adam.

All this Jesus is for us sinners. All his life was one mission which addresses itself to us. As man, Jesus gives himself totally to men as brothers. He comes among them in their misery and pain, listens to their questions and gives them the word that pardons, heals and gives the eternal life they so thirst for. He eats with sinners and tells them of his love for them and it is for this reason that he has been sent by the Father among men. In the goodness of his human nature, he breaks down the walls which artificially separate men and Jesus creates thereby a union which was not present before. In all things he is the revelation of the heart of the love of God, good towards all. As Son, he became incarnate in order to be among men, he who is the perfect reflection of the love of the Father. Who sees him and believes in him, sees the Father, for by opening his heart to the absolute goodness of Jesus, man finds divine love.

The mission of the Son of Man goes so far that he destroys hate itself and the loneliness of men. He became obedient unto death as proof of that love. In his generosity he accepted the end of disobedient men and drank this challice even to its last dregs. By this very fact he changed the very sign of death. Even Christ's feeling of abandonment by God on the cross became the means for men to find him. Death is now the door of life and the acceptance of supreme abandonment (death) is the gesture which expresses union with God. His goodness, his patience among sinners, his resurrection for us—are all the *signs* of divine grace which searches for sinners to save them from the night of death due them for their sins.

Jesus is the man who enters fully in union with God and his brothers. He gives himself totally with no reserve, being thus the one in whom peace and union are found. He is the perfect, perfected man in his total surrender to God and to his brothers.

His whole existence—his life, death and resurrection—are one great event of perfect reconciliation
of all men to God.

Thus Christ is the great sacrament of God: he is
the sign that the redemptive love of God is realized
among men, the divine action which operates for
men and among men. As the *Constitution on the
Church* says:

> Just as the assumed nature inseparably united to the
> divine Word serves him as a living instrument of sal-
> vation, so, in a similar way, does the communal struc-
> ture of the Church serve Christ's Spirit who vivifies
> it by way of building up the body (par. 8).

The humanity of Jesus is an instrument, but it
is "animated"; he is a real man who is really the
Son of God. His action incarnates the word of the
Father and gives him a palpable presence among
men: "That which was from the beginning, which
we have heard, which we have seen with our eyes,
which we have looked upon and touched with our
hands, concerning the Word of life," (1 Jn 1:1). This
means that the one who finds the man Jesus, who
has faith in him and places his hope in him, en-
counters the salvific power of God which works
salvation in him.

Considered from this central focus the Church
is also to be conceived as a sacrament. We could
arrive at this conclusion by starting from the doctrine of the Church as the mystical body of Christ.
In biblical language, "body" signifies the whole

man in his sensible and empirical form in such a way that the Church, terrestrial body of the glorified Lord, is nothing other than the permanent and visible presence of the glorified Lord in time and space. In fact, as the Constitution says, "it is he who vivifies the members of the Church; they are led by him, their head, and his spirit elevates them to communion with him and among themselves" (par. 7).

One could also start with the premise that the Church is the salvific work of God on earth. In the words of Clement of Alexandria:

> As the will of God is a work which is called the world, his decree is to the salvation of men and is called the Church. (*Paedagogus*, I, 6)

At this point we ought to investigate and develop the images that the Constitution borrows from Sacred Scripture. The Church is a house constructed by God where redeemed humanity lives which is the family of God and the temple which serves him; it is a field which God sows and fertilizes; it is his bride whom he brings to his Son that she might be the mother of many children (par. 6). These images and many like them which were very common in both the patristic and scholastic periods, have heavily influenced the thought of the Church. They picture the Church as a sign under which is manifested the salutory grace of Christ; the Church is pictured as a means or instrument which Christ uses to bring about his eternal plan. That is why the *Constitution on the Church* can call the Church a sign, a sacrament and an instrument of salvation (par. 1). But in putting the two terms "sign" and "instrument" on the plane, we see only very imperfectly the mysterious connection which characterizes the nature of a sacrament. It is a divine action, the work of the Spirit and at the same time a visible rite, a realization which tending towards its consummation, is at once the result and the instrument of the salvific action of God, the actualization which, while remembering the terrestrial ministry of Jesus, turns the spirit towards the glorified Lord while awaiting his return.

The *Constitution* says that the Church has this complex nature of a sacrament. It is "the instrument of redemption" (pars. 9, 33) but an instrument which refers fundamentally to the Spirit of the Lord. This is the essential argument of par. 8. The Church is therefore an instrument in which Christ lives, which he animates with his Spirit and whose face reflects the traits of Christ and the light of God destined for men (par. 50). That means that the Church is more than an instrument or a servant. It is already, in a certain fashion, the effective salvation and regeneration of humanity itself according to the model of its creator (par. 48). The Church already manifests the definitive unity of the elect and serves it by signifying it (par. 11). In the Church's life we anticipate in a sense our celestial joy (par. 51). All these affirmations certainly express—better than the lapidary terms of "sign and sacrament"—its correlation to salvation. It is this which was richly expressed by primitive Christianity when it used the terms *mysterion-sacramentum*. More than a simple instrument of salvation, the Church is thus "the germ and the beginning of the Kingdom" (par. 5). She is the chosen people of God for the eternal alliance and as St. Augustine says, of reconciled humanity. She is thus the revelation—hidden but real—of the glorified Lord. She is the means and the sign of salvation because she constitutes the beginning of this salvation.

In the beginning, the Church appeared essentially as the society of the friends of Christ, that is, of those who loved Christ and were loved by him and who, out of love of him, loved each other. The Church is essentially a fraternity and a charity. We belong to it by faith (and baptism) and by our whole person. No one can belong to the Church without knowing it—at least in some way. That means that the Church is a community which implies the profound personal adherence of the self— "a community of faith, hope and charity" (par. 8) or a "communion of life, of charity and of truth" (par. 9).

It is Christ Jesus who assembled men around himself. The gospels as well as the *Acts of the Apostles* show this clearly. The center of the

Church is formed by the twelve called by Jesus "to be his companions" (Mk 3:13–19; Lk 6:12–16; Jn 1:42–51). Belonging was the result of Christ's initiative and his choice (Jn 15:16). It was a gift, which in the measure in which Jesus reveals himself ever more clearly, appears as a true grace of God, for the union with the Son implies union with the Father. As with every human society, the Church also depends on the response of men. Jesus proposes and men give their consent by affirming that he is prophet and after the death and resurrection, the Lord. That means that they believed firmly in the mystery of God which is revealed in Jesus Christ.

At Pentecost this nucleus of the primitive Church becomes a germinal cell. The Apostles preach the good news: "God has made him Lord and Christ" (Acts 2:36). Many accepted him and were consequently baptized (Acts 2:41, 47; 5:14; 11:24). These disciples believed that they were the holy people of God whom God assembled in the power of the Spirit. In fact, it is reunited and maintained by the testimony they render of Jesus and by the faith in him.

This testimony, inspired by the Holy Spirit of the great work of salvation which God accomplished for all in Jesus and the response of faith which, infused by the Holy Spirit, both continually construct the Church and give it its interior unity. The Church believes and professes that her essential unity is a gift of the Holy Spirit who gives to the entire body "its life, unity and movement" (par. 7). It is the Spirit who realizes the accord between the qualified testimonies and the believing people and yet are all in communion one with another (par. 13). Even the solidarity of the hierarchical structure rests in the last analysis on this gift of the Spirit (par. 27).

This doctrine essentially implies the effective permanence of the salvific work of Jesus Christ, for, even if it happened in the historical past, it has an eternal value. This means that the Church teaches, baptizes, celebrates the Eucharist as a continuation of the mission it has received in the beginning. It follows that in the essential action of the Church, in the work of her ministry, the Lord is truly there in the midst of her and that he directs her himself by the mysterious conjugation of the Word and of the mission given to the Apostles on the one hand, and on the other by the impulsion of the Holy Spirit.

The heart of the Church is the salvific work of God, accomplished for all men by the death and resurrection of Christ and addressed as a continuous sign among men. This work is the object of faith: in baptism, which gives the quality as member, it is given to a particular person; in the Eucharist, the vital center of the Church, it is not only represented in a symbolic sense but effectively actualized (par. 28). The human society which is the

Church is a union which is born of this work, is constantly being constituted until the time when redemption is completely accomplished for all of humanity. In its existence as a society fully human, that is, in its proclaiming, its administration of the sacraments, its government confided to qualified leaders and its free obedience, the Church is the visible and powerful presence of the salvific action of God. It manifests itself with force in its reality and its life.

From this theological conclusion, we can easily see how the efficacy of the other sacraments repose in the participation which they have in the ecclesial society, for, being a situation in the Church, each sacrament is also a situation of grace.

II

The Council thus calls the Church "sacrament" only because it is Christ himself who is the fundamental sacrament and efficacious sign of God's love for all men. Christ is the sacrament of God insofar as he is the union of the divine and the human in the hypostatic union. In the mind of God, the redemption of the whole human race is envisioned by and through the Incarnation of Christ, who thus becomes the sign that God has received and loved all men in love in Christ. All men are thus "in Christ" in the sense that by the Incarnation, Christ united himself with our nature and became one race and one family with all men, past, present and future because of the universal salvific will of God.

Thus, there is not now and never was (in the intention of God) a purely "natural" order, until Christ, who then elevated us by grace to the "supernatural" order. Creation and redemption (grace) are two movements in the salvific will of God, united in the Incarnation of the Son of God and in which now all men are directly related in all of their decisions and orientations. Thus the culmination of God's will to save men is Christ, the Incarnate Word, who in time and space (history), shows men this love and mercy of God for all men. The Incarnation is the radical sacrament of God among us, for all time, insofar as in Christ God shows us his love and accepts us for all time into his forgiving mercy. Thus Christ is the visible sign (sacrament) in space and time of the real and present victory of God over death and sin, the promise and first fruit of our resurrection as well as of eschatological hope for all men. The Incarnation is the efficacious sign and sacrament of man's hope which appeared in history, at a particular time and place and not in obscure or hidden ways—which was the case before the historical moment of the Incarnation. This sacrament of God's love and mercy is not and cannot be provisional (as was the case in the "sacraments" of the old law) since the hypostatic union is permanent and forever (as the

Creed puts it: "He is seated at the right hand of the Father").

If we have understood why the Incarnation of Christ is now called the radical sacrament by both the Fathers of the Church and Vatican II, it should be clear why the Church is also called the primary sacrament from which all the seven sacred signs flow, as from a source. The reason is simple: the Church is sacrament only in Christ because in Christ all men are radically orientated to God by and through the hypostatic union. The human nature of Christ is divinized by this union and in God's intention, all men are now called to salvation only in and through Christ. The Church is the continuation in space and time of Christ's redemption and message to and for the whole world, for all time, because by the hypostatic union all men are radically and forever united or orientated to God through Christ.

Thus the Church is the historical appearance of God's grace which is given to all men in every age and excludes no one. The Church is the visible sacrament of what God intends for all men, now and in eternity which is the union of all men in a loving community which is called the Church. Thus, it is in the Church that the permanent grace and mercy of God appears now in space and time. She can then be called the permanent presence, the sacrament, the historically visible manifestation of

God's love and mercy for all men. The Church is at once the people of God as well as a socially organized community which can be seen by men. Salvation comes to the individual by entering the Church where Christ meets him in giving him what the Church is: the presence of the redemptive grace of Christ in space and time.

Thus, the Church is sign and sacrament for the whole human race since she carries within her at all times this message and grace of mercy and love. The Church as sacrament is permanent and for all men since God has willed to accept all men in and through the Incarnation of His Son. She is the radical sacrament from whom all the other seven sacred signs take their efficacy. The hypostatic union has brought the world into historical and social relationship with the whole family of men. This work of salvation is continued in space and time by the Church.

The Church is indeed hierarchically structured by the will of Christ, but this cannot take away the fact that we are all the Church. Each Christian in that sense is then also a sign and sacrament in the world, a continuation in space and time of Christ's mercy and love. Christians are Christ's sacrament insofar as through and in them, the Spirit of Christ can overcome the division, hatred, violence, war, injustice in the modern world. Thus Christians are or should be the explicit sign or sacrament of God's intention for the whole world: the union of all men in Christ which is the very definition of the Church.

READINGS

1. L. Cerfaux, *The Church in the Theology of St. Paul* (New York, 1964).
2. K. Rahner, *The Church and the Sacraments* (New York, 1963).
3. E. Schillebeeckx, *Christ the Sacrament of the Encounter with God* (New York, 1963).
4. O. Semmelroth, *Church and Sacrament* (Notre Dame, Ind., 1965).
5. A. Vonier, *The Church and the Sacraments*, II, *Collected Works* (Westminster, 1952).

DISCUSSION QUESTIONS

1. What is the Hypostatic union?
2. In what way are all men (at least potentially) saved in Christ?
3. How can we say that the Church is a "sacrament"?
4. In what way is the Church both a human as well as a divine reality?
5. In what way can we say that each Christian is a sacrament?
6. Can you give a definition of the Church?
7. What is the work of the Holy Spirit in the Church?

CHAPTER III

Baptism

Baptism is the sign of an individual's integration into Christ and the Church. As we have pointed out in Chapter Two, the Church is the fundamental sacrament because it is the continuation in space and time of the victorious and loving grace of Christ. The Church is the unfailing sign of this love and mercy as well as its effective presence. The individual is integrated into Christ (and therefore into God's saving action) by being integrated into the Church in the rite of initiation called baptism. In this act the Church actualizes herself, that is, shows herself to be what she is for *this* individual by integrating him by the "washing and the word" (as baptism was known in the early Church) into the body of Christ which the Church truly is. The sacred sign of baptism is therefore essentially ecclesial in nature for the simple reason that the Church, as the body of Christ in the world, is the

efficacious sign of Christ's saving power in space
and time. There can be no baptism in Christ without being by that very act an integration into the
body of Christ, the Church.

Thus, in the words of Tertullian, baptism is "the
conscious and blessed beginning of the Christian
life, a new birth and a rebirth in the image of
Christ." From the earliest testimonies of Christian
tradition, baptism was seen to be the beginning
and the foundation of Christian discipleship and
Christian existence. It was at this moment that the
Church met the person and communicated to him
Christ's grace and new birth and it is for that reason that we can call it a sacrament. This is what
was meant when the Apostles baptized "in the
name of Christ." Baptism was at once an act of
faith and penance in the recipient (so as not to con-
fuse it with a magical rite which was so common
in the pagan rites of initiation) and a creating act
in Christ whereby sins were forgiven, a new creation (grace) was given as well as the gift of the
Spirit. It is this light of Christ and new creation in
Christ to which the person professes belief in accepting this undeserved grace of and from Christ.
Thus baptism—like all the other sacred signs in
which Christ's redemption becomes actualized for
us here and now, in this moment of human history
in Holy Church—is a profession of faith and not a
magical formula. It is, on the part of him who receives this grace, an explicit and personal "yes" to

this whole historical manifestation of God's mercy and love in Christ. The early Church presupposed that as a regular process, only adults were baptized. Children were baptized from the earliest days but this poses a special theological problem which we will discuss briefly later.

The scriptures describe baptism as an efficacious sign of Christ's death and resurrection worked in the baptized here and now: "You were buried with him in baptism, in which you were also raised with him through faith in the working of God, who raised him from the dead" (Col 2:12). Baptism is then, according to St. Paul, an imitation of Christ, in which the death and resurrection of Christ are efficaciously applied to this person in time, thus giving him a new birth, a new creation (grace) in Christ. The symbolic washing is an efficacious symbol, that is, there is given to the baptized a real access to Christ and his redemption. The baptized thus truly die and rise with Christ, so that becoming like him in the likeness of His death, they may be like him in the resurrection (Phil 3:10). The going down into the water was likened to a death (since, for the ancients, water was a sign both of washing and of death) and the rising from the water likened to a resurrection from the dead.

Thus baptism as sign and symbol connotes two aspects, both received in faith, The first is the fellowship with Christ and the new life (grace) which is ours *now* as reality and as radical hope for the future. This new creation is given to us in baptism as a token and sign of the fullest revelation of our sonship on the last day, in the *Parousia* of Christ when the Lord returns.

All this the believer must personally and intelligently accept as really his not only for the moment but for the totality of his existence. Faith makes this a reality for this individual but baptism also implies that he make it the cornerstone of his whole life. Baptism then can be seen as a total consecration of the whole life of the Christian as well as (as its negative aspect) a death to the life of selfishness and sin. The whole Christian life must therefore show the existence of this new life in Christ. The baptized can then be said to be a "royal priesthood" not only in cultic service but in the liturgical service of their whole lives now consecrated and elevated by their new birth in Christ Jesus. Christians live this new life now in Christ and in the shadow of faith but also in charity (the sign of the presence of Christ in us) and in firm hope for the future when our sonship of God in Christ will be fully manifest in the final coming of Christ. To conclude: baptism is the symbolic action whereby the redemption of Christ, that is, his death and resurrection, are given to us here and now, giving us the beginning of Christian life by a concrete, visible and symbolic confession of faith which makes us like the crucified and risen Lord.

The baptized person thus dies with Christ and rises with him to new life in Christ in the hope of the future full glory of the resurrection. The whole of the life of the baptized is thus marked with death to selfishness and sin and life in a continuous act of love toward God and the neighbor. In this way, the royal priesthood of the faithful is actualized and made real.

Baptism of desire—for those who through no fault of their own have not heard and/or received the message of Christ—is also directly related to the saving grace of Christ. For since Christ became one in race and family with all men of all ages by the hypostatic union; and since in the mind of God the Incarnation is primary for salvation for all men; and since, moreover, God's saving grace is always working in all men, all of their willful actions are now in fact, consciously or unconsciously, orientated to their last end who is God. There can be no humanly willed action which is not so orientated, due to the positive will of God in saving all men in Christ. It follows that the whole of human life—by the positive will of God for salvation—is grace filled and orientated to salvation. All are thus called to salvation in Christ because all are radically orientated to Christ in the Incarnation. The actions of men done in freedom and in time—whether good or bad—orientate each and every man to eternal life or eternal death.

It also follows that baptism, once given, cannot
be repeated since there is only one orientation to
God, explicitly symbolized and given in baptism
(the scholastics called this the "indelible character
of baptism"). This of course does not mean that a
person cannot be unfaithful in part (lack of charity) or in total (lack of faith as in apostasy), but
only that God's promise and gift remain forever in
act even if, by infidelity, a person does not actualize this gift for himself. God continues to love even
when this love is rejected or treated lightly by
man. That is why we can say that the "baptismal
character" remains—not in any material sense—
even when the person has rejected his baptism:
the promise and love of God remains even in the
face of man's sin.

The same can be said of the baptism of children.
The omnipotence of God's grace is a total triumph
in this little baby because God saves each man as
he finds him, not as each man must first become,
before God finds him (the heresy of Pelagianism
or semi-Pelagianism). There is, however, at least
some faith in the reception of baptism by children,
and that is the faith of the Church, represented by
parents, godparents, etc. The Church is the essential sacrament of faith by the Incarnation of Christ.
Thus baptism remains valid both for the child and
the apostate because of God's omnipotent and
grace-filled call—even if the person will not (apos-

tate) or cannot (child) accept this call personally.
In the first case, baptism remains without the fruit
of grace because the apostate willfully rejects that
grace; in the second, the child is filled with grace
because of the faith of the Church which is always
believing.

It must in consequence also be noted that baptism—like all the seven sacred signs—remains of
itself efficacious not because of some magical formula or power, but because this sign is, by the will
of God, here and now a manifestation of God and
his salvific will which is taking place. These signs
are the abiding promise of God to offer his grace
and is recognizable and historically manifest here
and now and which cannot, on the part of God,
fail (*ex opere operato*). They do not and cannot
work like magic since the personal faith of the re-
ceiver is presupposed and demanded—otherwise
there can be no sacrament, properly speaking.
That is why St. Thomas always spoke of the *sacra-
menta fidei* (sacraments of faith) because no word
and ritual can be efficacious for this man at any
historical moment without a loving "yes" on the
part of free man who receives free grace. But because of the Incarnation of the Son of God who remains forever by his death and resurrection the
tangible and visible offer of grace in the Church
is forever and without end. This stable promise of
redemptive grace in Christ is the reason we can

say that baptism—like all the sacraments—is efficacious of itself in the Church to him who approaches these signs of grace with love and faith.

READINGS

1. *Adult Baptism and the Catechumenate,* ed. J. Wagner (New York, 1967: Concilium series, vol. 22).
2. Y. Congar, *Wide World, My Parish* (Baltimore, 1961).
3. J. Jerimias, *Infant Baptism in the First Four Centuries* (London, 1958).
4. P. F. Palmer, *Sources of Christian Theology* I *Sacrament and Worship* (Westminster, Md., 1956).
5. R. Roper, *The Anonymous Christian* (New York, 1966).
6. H. Schlette, *Toward a Theology of Religions* (New York, 1966).

DISCUSSION QUESTIONS

1. What is baptism in the Church?
2. Why do we say that baptism is a new birth?
3. What is the relationship between baptism and the Church?
4. How does St. Paul describe baptism?

5. Is baptism a magic formula? Explain.
6. Why should small children be baptized?
7. What is the grace of baptism?
8. What is the relationship between baptism and the rest of life?
9. What is the "royal priesthood" of the faithful?

CHAPTER IV

Confirmation

From the very earliest days of the Church, the sacrament of confirmation was looked upon as the complement and fullness of baptism, so that together they constituted the initiation into Christian existence. As a matter of historical fact, in the early Church when most of those initiated into Christianity were adults,[1] both of these sacraments

[1] The normal rite of Christian initiation was, in the early Church, restricted to adults since only they were considered capable of responding to the call of God's grace in freedom. All of the rituals which have come down to us from this period are specifically related to adults. Not much thought was given to the baptism of children until the time of St. Augustine and the controversies concerning original sin. Children, however, were in fact baptized but this was always done within the community of faith which is the Church and the "small" Church which is the family. It was only within this intensely lived life of faith with the family that baptism was ever permitted to be given to children and as an extension of that small community of faith. In such a context, all semblances of ritualism or formulism as regards infant baptism was by definition excluded.

were administered together. It is difficult to find much theological thought by the early and middle writers of the Church concerning this sacrament. What was emphasized was that confirmation was the Pentecost of each of the baptized to enable them to bear witness to the faith in the world. Therefore what is clear even from the earliest days was the relationship between the Spirit and confirmation.

The Acts (2:1–47; 8:12–17; 10:1–20; 19:1–7, etc.) gives us a clear teaching on the Pentecost gift of the Spirit to the faithful. Just as Christ received the mission from the Father to go into the world to save it by announcing the presence of the kingdom of God (Incarnation) so too the Church as well as each of her members is now given the mission to do so by "the consecration and anointing of the Spirit" (as confirmation was known in the early Church). This divine anointing was a spiritual quality given to the Christian to sustain his whole spiritual life; it was the action of God in arousing faith in the hearts of those who are obedient to the Word of God. The scriptures tell us that it is the Spirit who is source of our love (1 Cor 13:1–13); of our prayer (Rom 8:16) as well as the source of all charisms or special gifts in the Church (1 Cor 12:4–12). All this is given so as to build up the Church (1 Cor 14:4, 12, 26), thereby consecrating it as the Temple of God (Eph 2:22); it is the Spirit who keeps the Church in unity and communion (Phil

2:1) and He is indeed the very soul of the Church (Gal 5:25; 6:9; Rom 8:9; 13; Eph 4:30). The New Testament scriptures view this gift of the Spirit in a different fashion from that given in baptism (even though these gifts are also present in this incorporation into Christ) and from the earliest times, this visible and public manifestation of the Spirit in the Church was signified by a distinct (though connected with baptism) rite known to us today as the sacrament of confirmation. Yet, even if we have seen this reality in light of scripture and tradition, this still has not given us a clear theology of this sacrament. In other words, what is the specific sign of this sacrament in the Church?

As we have seen above in our study of the scripture, the Church in general and each of the faithful in particular, in receiving the gift of the Spirit, receive the various *carismata* or gifts of the Spirit for the edification and building up of the presence of the Church in the world. In other words, each of the baptized faithful, in receiving the Spirit of confirmation in faith, receive a special gift or charism (St. Paul lists many of them in his epistles, given by the Spirit for the good of all not just the one who receives them) *for the sake of others*, and finally for the building up of the whole Church in the world.

This "world" must be taken in the scriptural sense of the word, both hostile and ignorant. Many times men are ignorant of God's word and come into contact with it by the good example of Christians. This is one way to bear witness to the Spirit and the gospel "in the world." Yet, often men are hostile to God's word as well as his emissaries in the world, Christians. Indeed, they may be persecuted and even killed for bearing witness to the gospel in their lives. It is for this reason that confirmation can be said to give the recipient "strength" in the face of adversary in bearing witness to Holy faith "in the world." Therefore, the use of the word "world" must be used with care for it can mean different things in different contexts.

We have also seen that God's grace active in each of the faithful has a double dimension. The one is the grace of dying with Christ, a death to sin, egoism, greed, selfishness and all the other aspects which kill and diminish love; but God's grace in Christ is also related to saving and transforming the world, just as the resurrection of Jesus did not destroy the once pain-filled body of Christ but transformed it through the passion and death. This mission to transform the world is the mission given to the confirmed since the mission is essentially related (charismatically) to others in the world. It gives the baptized the strength and spiritual force to become the visible sign of Christ's presence in the world that men in the world may see (i.e. the works of love) and wonder as men once wondered when they saw the first Christians love each other so deeply. Each of the faithful has his own vocation and his own carism to work out this mission of Christ's presence in the world (v.g. alms giving, hospitality, teaching, reconciliation, etc.). It is the sacrament of confirmation which confers this charismatic Spirit who confers the mission to witness to as well as transform the world in the Spirit of Christ.

It is precisely at this point that we must place the whole theology of the Christian apostolate to and for the world. The Church, as we have seen, radically encompasses the whole human family. It therefore follows that "the joys and hopes, the griefs and the anxieties of the men of our age, especially those who are poor or in any way affected, are the joys and the hopes, the griefs and the anxieties of the followers of Christ" (*Pastoral Constitution* of Vatican II, par. 1). Christians are intimately and inextricably united with all men in the one act of redemption in Christ. The whole of human life has been elevated by the Incarnation and resurrection of the Son of God. The "world" then—that is, the locus of the joys, pains, hopes and sorrows of all men—is the place where the Christian shows his preeminent love of God and the brother, in relating and doing, concerning these needs of the men of each age. Therefore the problems of poverty, civil and human rights, prison reform, the aged, war and peace, political action, etc., are as much a part of the cultic reality for the

Christian as the celebration of the Eucharist. The sacrament of confirmation strengthens us for this task *for others*.

As we have seen elsewhere, the Church is the historical presence of God's loving mercy and love in the world. She has the same mission as the Father gave to Jesus; and just as God did not abandon the world to its own nothingness and despair, so too now (and in every age), with the Church. So the Church is actualized and efficaciously symbolized in the sacrament of confirmation in each of the faithful who thereby receive this mission of Jesus to save the world and to transform it by his work within it.

The result of this sacrament then is not that the individual who receives it is strengthened in his own faith, but rather to strengthen him for the apostolate to the world, for this sacrament is essentially related to others. Confirmation is the symbolic but efficacious sign of the Christian's participation in the mission of the Church to the world. Insofar as each of the faithful work to transform the world—in whatever way and to whatever extent—they bring about in their lives the grace and love of the Church (and therefore of Christ) for the world. For Confirmation is above all and essentially the charismatic gift of the Spirit *for others* who thereby are not abandoned to despair but are given hope.

READINGS

1. M. Bohen, *The Mystery of Confirmation* (New York, 1963).
2. Y. Congar, *Lay People in the Church* (Westminster, Md., 1957).
3. G. Dix, *The Theology of Confirmation in Relation to Baptism* (Westminster, 1946).
4. B. Neunheuser, *Baptism and Confirmation* (New York, 1963).
5. P. F. Palmer, *Sources of Christian Theology. I. Sacraments and Worship* (Westminster, Md., 1956).
6. L. Thornton, *Confirmation: Its Place in the Baptismal Mystery* (Westminster, 1953).

DISCUSSION QUESTIONS

1. In what way is confirmation a complement and fulfillment of baptism?
2. Is it correct to say that confirmation makes us "soldiers of Christ"?
3. At what age ought confirmation to be given?
4. What is the reason for confirmation?
5. How does the New Testament view the Holy Spirit?
6. What is the specific sign of confirmation?
7. What do we mean when we say "the world"?
8. What is the nature of the Christian apostolate to the world?

CHAPTER V

The Eucharist

The sacrament of the Eucharist was seen by the first Christians as the very heart of the Church and indeed, the Church itself is actualized or came to be in its saving reality in the breaking of the bread. The early writers of the Church claimed that *Eucharistia facit ecclesiam* ("the Eucharist creates the Church"). The reason is simple: this sacrament contains the very source of salvation, Christ, the crucified and risen Lord, by whom alone the Church comes into existence and in which, alone, the faithful can find salvation.

From the earliest days of the Church—as attested to by all of the gospels and the epistles of St. Paul—the Eucharist was celebrated. The word "eucharist" comes from the Greek, *eucharistein* which means to give thanks for a precious gift. For in the Eucharist, the first Christians gave thanks for the most precious gift of all possible gifts, that is, for the very source of salvation, Jesus. The redemption mystery of Jesus was actualized and brought about in the act of celebrating the Eucharist (cf. Lk 22:19; Mk 14:23; Mt 26:27; 1 Cor 11:24). It is Christ himself (the source of the Church and of all the other sacraments as extensions of the mystery of the Church) who is actualized and made present in the action and words of the sacrificial meal called the Eucharist. In other words, in the Eucharist, what we have is the presence of the salvific reality called Jesus by means of the uttered thanks of the Church through the words of God uttered over the bread and wine. The saving Christ is actualized in our midst by and in the Eucharist which creates, strengthens and unifies the Church.

As we have already said, the celebration of this sacrament goes back to the earliest days of the Church. We see this in the witness of St. Paul's epistle who in his own turn, in relating to the Christians a tradition which he himself had received from the Church (1 Cor 11:23–28). The epistle was written in the early fifties of our era (52 A.D.) and since St. Paul refers back to an even earlier tradition which he himself had received from the Church, we can see how old was the celebration of the Eucharist in the Church. Indeed, each of the gospels records the institution of the Eucharist at the Last Supper (with the exception of St. John who gives us his Eucharistic teaching in chapter six of the gospel), and although each of the sacred authors emphasize various theological themes, the basic meaning of the reality of the Eucharist as meal, offering, sacrifice and expiation, remains the same in all four gospels. This is seen from an examination of these sources of the Eucharistic tradition in the Church. It must be remembered, moreover, that the gospels are nothing else than the most primitive practice and belief of the Church itself. In other words, the Church created the gospels, not vice versa.

The mission of Jesus from the Father was to save men from sin, to become expiatory sacrifice for the sins of all men (by his death) so as thereby to become the principle of salvation when this sacrifice was accepted by the Father (resurrection). The suffering and death of Jesus was a consciously willed suffering and death for the sins of the whole world and not simply a fatuous happening of nature or result of the malice of men. Jesus is a free and consciously willed expiation for the sins of the whole world. He died and endured the death which all men must endure since death is a sign of sin itself. He suffered the loneliness, abandonment by God and the sufferings of death itself so that by dying and rising (the acceptance by the Father of the person and work of Jesus), he was able to change the ambiguity of death from a sign of death in sin to a sign of death to sin—the very reality of eternal life. It was in his death willingly and lov-

ingly endured that Jesus attains the fulfillment of
his being and by rising, he attains the fulfillment of
his supreme role of Savior of all men (Rom 1:4). In
his death, Jesus gives himself completely to the
Father as expiatory sacrifice for the sins of all men
and the Father accepts this gift—no longer in the
form of things such as goats and bulls, but in the
form of the very work and person of Jesus—in and
by the resurrection. Jesus is thus constituted forever as glorious Savior of all men. Access to God
can only come in and through the incarnate and
risen Son of God, Jesus Christ.

The Last Supper offered by Jesus was the new
testament or covenant of all of this salvific reality
for men offered symbolically but divinely efficacious by the divine words of Jesus. In other words,
the meal of the Last Supper was a prophetical action, that is, it was the actual realization of the divine decree already and present now in the act of
the pascal meal. The words of Christ ("This is my
body," "This is my blood") bring about efficaciously what is symbolized by this meal of eating
and drinking. The meal is thus an efficacious sign
of what Jesus did at his passion, death and resurrection.

This is seen clearly in the text of sacred scripture. The Eucharist is a true expiation for sin
which is "given for many" (Mk 14:24). It is a sacrifice given for the sins of all men, not for a chosen
few or for "the elect." The text here is a clear al-

lusion to the suffering servant of Yahweh theme in Isaiah 53:12 where the innocent servant suffers as expiation for the sins of the people. The death of Jesus at the meal is symbolized by the separate words directed and uttered over the two elements of bread and wine, indicating the separation of the blood from the body of Jesus offered on the cross. Even in the act of eating, the symbolic gift of Christ is symbolized. That is, as the food is totally consumed and goes for the sustenance of life, so too is Christ given for each one of us totally for our sustenance into eternal life. The meal then is identical with Christ's work on the cross. All of this was given by Jesus at the Last Supper as an efficacious sign, that is, by the omnipotent words of Jesus, what is symbolically enacted in the meal is really brought about in participating in the meal. It is for this reason that we can call the Eucharist the source of all the other sacraments.

Thus in the Eucharistic meal Jesus is present as Savior, that is, the Incarnate Word who by his sacrificial death brings about the salvation of all men. Jesus also commands the Church to do the same thing as he did: "Do this in memory of me." This "memory" must be taken in the biblical and liturgical sense of reenacting by the divine command what was once done for the salvation of all and which now, in this place and at this time (by the divine power and will) also becomes a living reality here and now. It is not the "memory" of just any event, but the memory of Jesus and what Jesus did, that makes this "remembering" efficacious by means of the divine power and words of Christ. By divine power, what Jesus did for us becomes reality for us in the celebration of the Eucharistic meal.

This realistic interpretation of the Eucharist was emphasized by all of the sacred authors but particularly by Sts. Paul and John. Paul states that the Eucharist is a true sharing in the very body and blood of Christ (1 Cor 10:16) and since all Christians partake of the same body, they are all radically one (*ibid.*, v. 17). This realistic interpretation goes as far as to condemn the one who eats of this bread in an unworthy manner (1 Cor 11:27–31).

St. John's teaching is also very realistic. Christ is the source of eternal life for all those who approach him in faith (6:26–47). He is the source of life not only because he is the Son but also because he died and rose for men which is now communicated to men in the Eucharist (6:51–58). Those who by faith participate in the Eucharist by that very fact participate in the passion, death and resurrection of Jesus since the Eucharist is intimately linked with the cross on which Christ gave his life for the life of the world (6:48–51). In receiving the Eucharist in faith, the Christian receives eternal life which prepares him for the resurrection on the last day. Yet, this life received from Christ is not just individualistic but above all communal (one could even say trinitarian) in its effects on the believer (vs. 56–57), since it puts him in relation to the Father (as well as the Son) who is the source of all life.

Thus the believer in the Eucharist lives in a profound community of love of the Father, Son and eventually in all of his believing brothers. All live for God and God lives in each one of the believers (Rom 14:7–9). Thus those who participate in the Eucharist receive the body and blood of the God-Man (the "Son of Man") and they receive it as a pledge of the final resurrection (6:54). This gift of eternal life in the Eucharist puts us in trinitarian union with the Father and the Son which thus forms a community of eternal love (6:55–57). We already share in this life of Jesus in the Eucharist with a firm *hope* and guarantee of our future resurrection. Each person as an individual lives this union with the Father and Christ. This is a remarkable development of the doctrine of the Eucharist. The ecclesial element is not explicitly brought out here (as in St. Paul) but it is implicitly contained in the notion of the community of eternal love with the Father and the Son.

All of this teaching from sacred scripture should make it very clear how the Eucharist is intimately and inextricably related to the Church. Being the very body of Christ and sharing in this body by all Christians, the very existence and unity of the Church is brought about in the celebration of the

Eucharist. Therefore the Eucharist should not be seen simply as a spiritual nourishment for the individual (it is certainly this) but nourishment insofar as the one who participates in the Eucharist is brought into deeper unity with the mystery of Christ and the Church. For it is in the Eucharist that the Church is actualized as redemptive mystery and when the individual participates therein, his redemption is also actualized but only insofar as he is thereby more deeply integrated into the mystery of the Church. It is for this reason that no mass can ever be a "private" mass but is, of its very nature as sacrifice and as meal, public event of the whole Church and in which the whole Church is present and actualized in redemptive mystery. Thus our participation in the one Eucharist body of Christ efficaciously brings about and gives a deeper part in the one body of Christ which is the Church.

As we have also seen from our short study of scripture, the Eucharist is essentially eschatological in nature as well, since it bears within it the very pledge of future, eternal life in the very source of eternal life, Jesus, that is, relates us to the end and consummation of our Christian existence. In this sense, the Eucharist is also the source of charity since Christ, the very expression of God has become Savior of men because of God's great love for men manifested at the appointed historical hour in Christ Jesus (cf. Titus 2:11; 3:4) and becomes the very heart of the Church since the

Church is the community of love, one with the trinity (cf. *Constitution on the Church,* par. 4). The same eating of the same body of Christ symbolizes and efficaciously realizes the very unity of the Church itself; it also symbolizes and efficaciously realizes the very source of love of the Church as well. Christ is present and visible in sacramental form creating, uniting and loving the whole church of God.

Thus the Church attains the greatest actualization of her nature in celebrating the Eucharist. It is—as we have seen above—the very sacrifice of Christ symbolized and efficaciously "remembered" in the Eucharist meal; it shows the various hierarchical orders in the Church in the visible sacrament of the priest with the people joined to him as the one people of God; it shows the essential nature of the Church which is one in Christ and wherein and by which all become one in Christ, offered and eaten as one bread; it is eschatological in direction since all who participate, share in the very bread and source of eternal life who is Jesus as pledge of eternal life; it is expiatory and penitential, since the Eucharist is offered for the sins of all men and where those who participate therein, pledge to make their own lives ones of penance of the Savior of men, Jesus. The Eucharist is the risen Lord, victory of God over sin and death and pledge of eternal life, who is operative and present in the Eucharist. Those who participate in this sacrament must thus become in their own lives the continuation in space and time (since they are the Church) for the salvation and service of others in the world. Christians become the living Eucharistic presence in the world by their own love and concern for the brothers. In the Eucharist, Christians are strengthened to bring about their royal priesthood among the nations as sign of God's redemption in the world.

READINGS

1. *The Breading of Bread*. ed., P. Benoit *et al*. (New York, 1969: Concilium series, vol. 40).

2. J. McGowan, *Concelebration: Sign of the Unity of the Church* (New York, 1964).

3. P. F. Palmer, *Sources of Christian Theology*. I *Sacraments and Worship* (Westminster, Md., 1956).

4. *The Sacraments: An Ecumenical Dialogue*. (New York, 1966: Concilium series, vol. 24).

5. R. A. Sarno, *Let us Proclaim the Mystery of Faith*. (Denville, N.J., 1970).

6. E. Schillebeeckx, *The Eucharist* (New York, 1968).

DISCUSSION QUESTIONS

1. What is the relationship between the Eucharist and the Church?

2. What do the Gospels teach concerning the Eucharist?

3. Why is the Eucharist called the "sacrament of unity"?

4. What is signified by the breaking of the bread, the separation of the bread and wine and the actual eating?

5. Why was the Eucharist called "the food of immortality"?

6. What is the relationship between the death-resurrection of Christ and the Eucharist?

7. In what way is the Eucharist both a meal and a sacrifice?

8. What do we mean when we say that the Eucharist is the source of all the other sacraments?

9. What is the relationship between the Eucharist and the Church?

10. How is the Christian a "eucharistic" presence in the world?

CHAPTER VI

Penance

The sacrament of penance and its practice is very ancient in the Church. Tradition speaks very clearly about the Church's power received from Christ to forgive sins of her children committed after baptism. Whatever else can be said of the evolution in discipline of this sacrament (and it has evolved greatly in history) what remains clear and without question is the consciousness of the Church to forgive in an authoritative way, all and every sin of the faithful (against the heresies of Montanism and Novatianism which attempted to limit the power of the Church over certain sins).

We may thus define the sacrament of penance as the efficacious application to *this* sinner at *this* historical moment; this integration of the sinner into the redemptive mystery of Christ is truly a remission of sins (negatively) and an application of grace (positively), of the redemptive passion and resurrection of Christ in and by the Church. Since sin is an offense against both God and the Church (insofar as by sin we reject God's call to love in Christ and consequently, since God's love is visibly and historically present in the Church as the Sacrament of Christ in the world, an offense against the Church as well), it follows that the sacrament of penance is an authoritative reconciliation by the Church of the sinner to both God and the Church (Vatican II, *Constitution on the Church*, par. 11) and admission to the communion of saints.

We have seen in what sense the Church is the fundamental sacrament of Christ, that is, the Church is the efficacious presence of God's saving and loving grace in the world in every age as the body of Christ. She is then the community of those who love and believe in the Lord Jesus, called to the forgiveness of sins and life and reconciliation with God. In baptism, the person baptized is incorporated into the Church, the body of Christ, and consequently by that very fact, this integration into the Church also becomes the efficacious sign of his life in Christ. So too in the sacrament of penance. The reconciliation of the sinner with the Church (represented in private confession by the duly authorized minister) is a visible and efficacious sign of the sinner's reconciliation with God as well, for it is only within the Church that the baptized sinner meets the forgiving word of God's mercy in history. It is for that reason that we can

call penance (both the acts of penance of the sinner
and the action of the minister as representative of
the Church) a true sacrament.

As is evident in history, Christians, even after
baptism, returned to their former sins. How were
they to be reinstated into the Church and into the
"life germ implanted by God" which they had lost?
Even from the earliest times, the Church was conscious of a power given her by the Redeemer himself to reconcile these fallen Christians to herself
and, by her, to Christ. By penance in union with
the Church, the sinner once again finds the peace
of the Holy Spirit. In this sense, the penance of the
Christian is sacramental in the Church where he
meets the actualization of the redemptive mystery;
it is efficacious only in union with the Church and
is then only accomplished in an ecclesial act. Christian penance is, therefore, a sacrament of Christ in
his Church. By the visibility of the "power of the
keys" given to the Church by Christ, that is, by the
actualization of the redemptive mystery in the
Church united with the sinner's own avowal of sin
and sorrow, the Christian is certain of his forgiveness and his reincorporation into Christ by and
through his reincorporation into the community of
salvation which is the Church. Visible in its ministry, visible in its avowal of sin by the penitent, the
sacrament of penance is the visible manifestation of
Christ's saving mercy in and through the Church.

The scriptures give this power of "binding" and

"loosing" to the Church (cf. Mt 18:17; Jn 20:19; 1 Cor 5:3, etc.) where Jesus confers on the Apostles (and only on them as leaders in the Church) his own authority of "loosing" sinners from the realm of the darkness of sin and death. The teaching is rather clear: the Church has been given the victorious and salvific power of Jesus over sin and death so that anyone who is reconciled with the Church on earth (in which this victorious and salvific power of Christ is always present) is by that very fact also within the domain of God's saving power and has therefore attained the true forgiveness of sins on earth in the name of God. This binding and loosing from the power of Satan to the forgiving grace of God, is truly an efficacious and rea! juridical power of the Church on earth. The early Church called this an "excommunication," that is, the sinner (for the purpose of salvation) is placed outside the saving action of the Church, so that by and after penance, the sinner thereafter is reconciled with the Church, readmitted into the domain of God's saving action which is the Church. The very reception of the sinner once again into the Church is the efficacious sign of both his forgiveness of his sins (negative aspect) and his reconciliation with God (grace, the positive aspect).

This reconciliation with the Church (called *pax ecclesiae* in the early Church) is the same today, although more hidden in the private manner in

which the discipline of this sacrament has come
down to us today. There is also an "excommunication" (not in the canonical sense) in the sense that
a person truly conscious of serious sin may not partake of the Eucharist. Reconciliation with the
Church (and therefore with God) comes about
when the repentant sinner (which is absolutely
necessary for the reality of this sacrament) comes
to the Church (in the presence of the duly authorized minister of the Church), asks pardon of God
and of the Church and receives the reconciliation
of the Church and of God. Both the acts of the
penitent and of the Church involve a consequence
(reconciliation both with the Church and God)
which is truly so before God. It is this divine reality which we call the sacrament of penance in the
Church.

It is also in this sense that we can say that the
act of sin in any of the faithful is both an offense
against God (a denial and rejection of God's merciful love) and the brothers (he has deprived them
of good example, communion of good works, spiritual deeds, etc., known as the *Communion of
Saints*). It is for this added reason, because of sin's
double dimension, that the sinner stands in need of
reconciliation both of the Church and of God.

In all of this, as we have stated but not fully ex-
plained, the acts of the penitent are vital for the
existence of the sacrament of penance. In other
words, the penitent must approach the Church in

a spirit of penance or, as the scholastics called it, with the virtue of penance. If it were otherwise, we would run the danger of juridicism or even of magic. The acts of the penitent, excited to penance by the always operative grace of God on every sinner to repent, are therefore an essential part of this sacrament. Yet, the virtue of penance, although essential for the sacrament, has a much broader connotation in the lives of the faithful since it encompasses the whole life of each of the faithful. It includes all those interior as well as exterior attitudes to sin, the danger of which is present throughout the mortal life of each of the faithful. The virtue of penance includes the courage to accept one's own sinful past and present without degenerating into a guilt of stricken state of mind leading to neurosis; penance excludes all boasting and self-righteousness since we know ourselves to be the object of God's saving mercy and love only because God is love and not that there is anything in us that attracts God to us; it includes the courage to accept our sinful past and the will to work for a better future by struggling against our selfishness, inconsiderations, greed, and unconcern for others; it means accepting the burden of the consequences of the sins of others and making reparation with Christ for the sins of the whole world (fasting, alms giving, mortification in all of its diverse forms, prayer, etc.); it means accepting the burden of ourselves as sinners as well as others along with the consequences of sin that we can see in the world around us: murder, hate, uncorn, war, selfishness, racism—and working to alleviate these conditions in the world as best we can. In this sense, the sometimes discouraging task of constructing the city of man because of the greed of most men, can be subject of great penance on the part of the Christian so as not to lead to discouragement and cynicism.

It is clear then that the virtue of penance is not simply restricted to receiving the sacrament of penance (it is this of course) but must encompass the whole life of each of the faithful. Indeed, we may see this virtue of penance in the light of the satisfaction that is required of us by God and the Church for the sins we have committed. Even our own lives are not—as long as we remain wayfarers on earth—completely integrated into God's merciful and loving grace given to us in baptism and regiven anew in penance. It is in this sense that the Church saw, even after the sacrament of penance was duly given the sinner, the residual effects and remains of sin in the penitent for which more penance always was demanded. This is so because the selfishness and cancer of sin has made deep inroads into the very depth of our human person, and thereby has entered and affected all the dimensions of our existence. In the light of what we have said above concerning the virtue of penance, it is clear to see how, just as the whole being of the sinner has been affected by his sin, so too by the practice of the virtue of penance throughout our lives, we permit God's mercy and love to enter ever more deeply into the very recesses of our being and existence. It is this grace of God received in the sacrament of penance which signifies the strength and the obligation to integrate our whole being which has been injured by sin into our new "yes" to God by a genuine exercise of penance so as to become ever more fervent in love. For in the last analysis, it is only by love and its intensification in our lives, that sin, any and all sin, is forgiven: "Because she has loved much, much is forgiven her."

READINGS

1. P. Anciaux, *The Sacrament of Penance* (New York, 1962).

2. P. DeRosa, *Christ and Original Sin* (Milwaukee, 1967).

3. P. F. Palmer, *Sources of Christian Theology.* II. *Sacraments and Forgiveness* (Westminster, Md., 1960).

4. S. Richter, *Metanoia: Christian Penance and Confession* (New York, 1966).

5. P. Riga, *Sin and Penance* (Milwaukee, 1963).

DISCUSSION QUESTIONS

1. In what way is penance communal?
2. What is the relationship between the sacrament of penance and the Church?
3. What is the sign of penance in the Church?
4. What is the "communion of saints"?
5. Why is it not surprising that we have had an evolution in the discipline of the sacrament of penance?
6. How can sin be an offense against both God and man?
7. What are the "power of the keys" of the Church?
8. What does it mean for the Church to "bind and loose" from sin?
9. Explain the "virtue" of penance.

CHAPTER VII

The Sacrament of Marriage

From the earliest days of her tradition, the Church was conscious of the special reality of Christian marriage (cf. Mt 5:27; Mk 10:11; Lk 16:18; Cor 7:39; Eph 5:18). Christian marriage (or marriage in Christ, as it was called), was certainly all that any human marriage was among the pagans, but it was, however, to be more profound insofar as it symbolized the Church itself in miniature form; and because it symbolized a moment of divine love and grace among men, it was from the earliest days considered to be what today we call a "sacrament." But how?

Much of Christ's teaching on marriage (Mt 19:9) referred directly to the text of *Genesis* (Gen 3:16) where marriage is seen to be a holy thing, something natural to man and created by God. Marriage is a reality so profound in man's mortal existence that he will leave every other relationship in order to become part of this fundamental community. The teaching of Genesis on marriage is at once nuanced and beautiful where man cannot be defined or understood except in function of woman and vice-versa. Adam's nature is the measure of Eve's nature (and vice-versa) with the result that it is the couple which is the sacred reality created by God for man. Marriage, therefore, of its very nature is a holy and natural state from the very creation of man himself.

The second text that had a great influence on the early Christians with regard their thinking on marriage was Ephesians 5:21–33. In this text, St. Paul sees marriage as a sacred reality because it reflects and symbolizes the marriage (or love) of Christ with the Church. The reality of marriage is based upon and is supposed to reflect this union and love of Christ for the Church. Marriage is in this way a supernatural event where the mutual love expressed between the couple (in all of its dimensions) is of itself elevated to and is a participation in the very love which Christ has for the Church. This as yet has not told us how marriage in the Christian dispensation is a true sacrament.

We have seen in previous chapters that in the order of God's mind and plan for the redemption of man, it was the Incarnation of Christ which is primary. Because of God's love and for no other reason, the Word became flesh to show men God's love and the way to God's love in visible and tangible form. Jesus is the historical revelation of God's love for man in visible appearance:

> And the Word became flesh and dwelt among us; and we saw his glory, the glory of the Only Begotten Son, full of grace and truth. (Jn 1:14)

By this very fact, because the Word becomes one race with humanity, the Church is born out of love. The whole life of Christ—from his Incarnation to his glorious death and resurrection—was (and remains always in and through the Church) the visible manifestation of God's love for men (the Church). This fundamental reality of God's love and mercy is the radical basis for the redemption of men. Christ, and following him, the Church, are the fundamental sacraments of God's victorious grace in history.

Marriage as a sacrament stands within this reality of love and mercy in time. The love which the partners have for each other is a participation, an actualization here and now, of the love of Christ and his Church. For the community which is established by the joining of this man and this woman, is a Church in miniature and when they love each other, they become the sign and symbol of the divine reality of love in their lives, thus constituting not an empty symbol, but a truly efficacious one which we call a sacrament. The attitude and relation of Christ to the Church is the radical model of love for the attitude and relation which must be brought about in the reality of marriage since Christian marriage objectively represents this love of God in Christ for the Church.

It is at this point that it is important to understand exactly what is the Christian reality of love, the heart of the redemptive and conjugal reality we are discussing. We have seen that a sacrament is the visible and historical manifestation of God's grace to man. Yet, the very heart of both the redemption and the mystery of human existence is the mystery of love itself who is God (1 Jn 3:8). Human love and divine love are not two generically different realities, but one reality. Indeed human love exists because it participates in the divine love. Love is man's opening to God in time (and eternity whose beginning is in time) as well as the very event of God's loving communication with man which we call grace.

In marriage, two human beings open themselves to each other only in and through love and become a loving "we." Married love is thus the actual practice of love of man (these two human beings) in giving each other to each other, in suffering with and for each other, in the death of selfishness and egoism, striving to live a human and loving existence together amid all the vissicitudes and joys of life. Marriage thus represents and symbolizes in its way (by love) the redemptive and loving act which Christ had (and has in the Church) for the Church. Christian marriage is thus

a miniature humanity and therefore a miniature
Church wherein men love and sacrifice for each
other out of love. The very unity and reality of
marriage is love for each other—which symbolizes
and brings about the Church's function among
men. Each Christian marriage is a sacrament precisely because it is a miniature Church and in
which the historical realization of the Church's
unity takes place, that is, in loving one another.
Any marriage, but more particularly Christian
marriage, then can never be simply a "secular"
reality because its substance is love and the event
of love and grace which not only unites men and
God but man with his fellow man. Each Christian
couple is a sign and symbol of love, which expresses the deeper and underlining reality of the
loving union of God and man. In marriage, the
Church becomes present in this tiny community of
redeemed mankind.

It is in this way that we can say that marriage is
a sacrament. When two Christians, a free man and
woman, consent to love each other forever in trou-
bles and in joys which characterize all of human
existence, this mutual love becomes an actualizing
symbol and sign of the Church in history and the
Church is thereby actualized in her essential loving function in *this* couple at *this* moment of redemptive history in their loving one another. The
reason is clear: in loving each other for better or
for worse, in sickness and in health for all days,

they in fact contribute to the union of Christ with
humanity, i.e. in this little community of humanity
at this precise moment in history. In their human
love which opens to the divine love, marriage creates the existence of the whole Church in miniature fashion as the grace-giving presence of God in
history.

Marriage is therefore a symbol and a sign, but
because it is based and created by love (when this
is present), it is an efficacious symbol of God's merciful love-grace in history. The sign and what is
symbolized are therefore united in marriage but
they must not be confused since we know that the
sign can be an empty sign in marriage, that is,
when there is no longer any more love informing
that marriage, what is symbolized is empty of
meaning. Therefore we can say truthfully that the
Church is present in marriage but only to the de-
gree that this marriage actually realizes its own
nature of loving communion, a loving "we" of redeemed humanity, that is, when this marriage is
sanctified by grace and lived in holiness. Thus the
sacramental sign of marriage can be said to be the
visible bond of ultimate, indissoluble love between
the partners until death and what it symbolizes is
true love and holiness lived in Christ which actualizes redemptive truth in this portion of redeemed
humanity here and now. Christian couples therefore by living a holy married life, by that very reality, participate in a salvific function. Marriage is

THE SACRAMENT OF MARRIAGE   71

therefore holy in its origins but only because it received its fullest expression and culmination in the redemptive will of God in the marriage of Christ with humanity by and through the Incarnation. Marriage brings two people into the mystery of redemption and for that reason can be called a sacrament.

This love within marriage also (by its very nature) opens the couple to the world in redemptive relationship. It is here that we meet the reality of the family as the natural expression and outcome of the love of the couple themselves. The begetting and education of children is the first encounter of this redemptive love of the couple with the world. As a continuation and incarnation of this love (sexual relations), the love itself becomes expression in the world by and in children and the family. This relationship of love to the world is so vital that even when it is not possible for a particular couple (v.g. age or infertility) this function must remain open to other outlets in the expansion of love. For the nature of marital love has also as one of its essential functions, to open this couple to others, whether children of their own or to other people. When this love is thereby communicated to the world, the sign itself of marriage is all the more intensified and growing. The sacrament of marriage is then open to the world, that is, as a sign of redemptive love to and for others. The very nature of true marital love should lead the couple

from themselves as a loving "we," to the communication of love to others (family, the world). In this
way, marital love should not and cannot become an
enclosed community (couple plus children) but an
opening of and by love to the larger community of
the Church.

READINGS

1. E. S. Geissler, *The Meaning of Parenthood* (Notre
   Dame, 1962).
2. C. P. Kindregan, *A Theology of Marriage* (Milwaukee, 1967).
3. M. Oraison, *The Human Mystery of Sexuality* (New
   York, 1967).
4. V. Pospishil, *Divorce and Remarriage* (New York,
   1967).
5. *The Sacraments in Theology and Canon Law* (New
   York, 1968: Concilium series, vol. 38).
6. E. Schillebeeckx, *Marriage: Human Reality and
   Saving Mystery* (New York, 1965).

DISCUSSION QUESTIONS

1. In what is the marriage of a believer and that of an
   unbeliever different?
2. What is the sign and symbol of Christian marriage?
3. Give the scriptural teaching on marriage (Old and
   New Testament).

4. What do we mean when we say that Christian marriage is based on Christ's love for the Church?

5. In what way is the sacrament of matrimony related to the Church?

6. What is the essential substance of any marriage?

7. Is it correct to call the family a "little Church"? How?

8. How can we distinguish love of God and love of man?

9. Explain: Love is man's opening to God in time.

10. Explain: Christian marriage is a miniature redeemed humanity.

CHAPTER VIII

The Sacrament of Orders

The sacrament of holy orders is intimately and inextricably united with the mission of the Church as Christ's presence in history. The reality of this sacrament is completely dependent upon the Church as historical and visible institution for the salvation of all men.

The early origins of this sacrament are unclear since the Church developed her life in different ways in different parts of the world. Even the terminology (v.g. cleric, priest, pontif, presbyter, minister, overseer, president) develops differently in different situations. What is clear, however, is that various functions within the Church were associated with a certain "order" in the Church as a service to the rest of the Church. The Church from the very beginning received certain men into this function for the service of the community.

The scriptures teach that Jesus entrusted a mission—the mission which He received from the Father, namely, to proclaim the presence of the Kingdom and to bear witness to the passion and resurrection of Christ—to "the twelve," a symbolic title envisioning the end of time (Mt 19:23; Lk 22:28–30). It was also confided to Peter in a special way as well (Mt 16:18). Yet we have a difficult time here in assigning a "special" mission to the Apostles and the successors appointed by them already in the New Testament, since there is but one mission given to the whole Church which obviously includes all of the faithful. Yet, it remains true that scripture describes with special insistency that the mission of the twelve is one of special "service" (Mk 9:35; 10:35; Mt 20:26–28). This mission includes above all the preaching of the Kingdom (Mk 9:32; Mt 10:10; Lk 9:46) which is given in John's gospel at the very end (20:19–23).

It should come as no surprise then that the development of this sacrament is slow as to its specific nature since it is inextricably included in the very mission of the whole Church. In other words, this sacrament is dependent upon the historical and visible sacrament of the Church as institution among men and since the organization of the local churches proceeded in somewhat different fashion and discipline, no clear cut development of the sacrament of Orders in the Church can be discerned with any regularity.

For, as we have already seen, whatever the

Church actualizes or brings about her essence—
which is her mission—it is at that point that we
have a sacrament and since the continuance of the
Church as historical institution of salvation is
willed absolutely by God, as the fundamental Sacrament of Christ in the world, every other sacrament must have been in her from the beginning.
Moreover, since the Church as historical institution has existed and must continue, the authority
of Christ's mission must always be with her as well
since otherwise the promise of Christ to the
Church to be with her all days to the end of the
world, would fall short of the mark. It is at this
point that we can begin to understand the sacrament of Orders (unless we are willing to say that
the authority of the Church appears charismatically in each new age, a proposition manifestly in
contradiction to the historical consciousness of the
Church).

This sacrament has been the object of definition
by many General Councils in the Church's history.
The Council of Trent, for instance, defined the essence of priesthood as "the power to consecrate,
offer and administer the body and blood of Christ
as well as to forgive and retain sins." But it is clear
from the context of this definition that Trent did
not want to give a complete doctrine of orders and
for that reason, remains open to further development in theology. Vatican II further developed the
theology of orders by emphasizing its Christologi-

cal and ecclesial context (*Constitution on the Church,* pars. 19–29; *On Holy Orders,* par. 2) in the light of the paschal mystery. The Council's teaching is that the episcopate is a true sacrament and the "fullness of the priesthood" in function of which the bishop is integrated into the episcopal college (with the pope) in order to rule, sanctify and teach the whole Church. Lesser orders of priesthood are in dependence and conjoined to the episcopate. Yet, we have not as yet actually seen why Orders are necessarily a sacrament.

The Church as we have seen, is the fundamental sacrament, that is, it is the community of a fellowship of faith and love united with their pastors and is the visible and efficacious sign of the living presence of the risen Christ in the world. God wills to save all men in Christ and it is the grace of the risen Christ which is offered to all men. But this grace and presence is signified and actualized by the Church which is part of the world. The Church is the mystery of salvation but it is also, inseparably, a historical and visible institution which must continue through space and time by the absolute will of God. In order for the sanctifying and saving power of Christ to be visible and actualized in the world, the Church is absolutely essential by the will of God and inclusive in this will, is also the transmission of Christ's power in men chosen by her in order to ever reconstitute herself anew in history. Christ's powers in an authoritative way (the power to teach and sanctify) is given in and through the sacrament of Orders in the Church.

How is the Church actualized in time? The Church embodies and actualizes or brings about her being above all in the Eucharist and the Word preached in order to nourish faith in her people. The mystery of salvation is proclaimed by the ministry in sacrament and in the preached word in the community of believers. Orders renders a man capable of this function within the Church and for the Church as a service to the Church. The priest is a sign within the community of believers since he is authorized by the Church in his ordination to stand before (as well as for) the people to act *in persona Christi* as an efficacious sign of Christ's presence within the community. This presence is seen in that the priest is a visible sacrament in the function given to him of sanctifying others, of preaching the faith as understood by the Church, in his liturgical prayer for men, in the consecration of the Eucharist which is the very heart and actualization of the Church itself. The priest is the symbol and efficacious sign of Christ's saving action in and by his ministerial function.

It is true that for all this to be accomplished in his ministry, a minister need not himself be holy. This is so because of God's fidelity in the offer of his grace in *this* sacramental act. This cannot be changed for the person who approaches with faith even if the minister is in a sinful condition. Therefore a sacramental function even when performed by an unworthy minister, is efficacious as to its end, namely, the sanctification of the one who approaches the sacrament with faith.

Yet, this cannot be the total story with regard the minister. As the Church teaches, the entrance of a baptized person into orders has as a necessary effect (to him who is freely and rightly disposed) a grace of holiness. The holiness of the Church exists in her members and outside of her members neither holiness nor the Church exists. If, by an impossibility, all the faithful were fallen away sinners, the Church would in fact cease to exist. The minister is essentially related to the mission of the Church as sign of Christ in preaching, sanctifying and teaching the holiness of Christ among men. It would be a complete defeat of orders if all ministers were, once again by an impossibility, fallen sinners. Therefore, the grace of Orders is directed to making ministers holy so that they can preach and proclaim this both in word and example to others in the Church. God's will to save and make holy remains always efficacious in the Church (even though we do not know exactly if we are holy at any one moment, and who are the actually holy ones on earth) and consequently, orders which are essentially related to the Church, must confer holiness since otherwise this would constitute a total defeat for the Church. Every minister bears witness to the faith of the Church in his life and words; by his function, he is essentially entrusted to give the testimony of holiness in his own life for the rest of the Church. This holiness is possible only through the grace of God and consequently this grace of holiness for the recipient flows from the very nature of the sacrament of Orders. The gift of ministry in and for the Church is therefore also a gift of grace to fulfill that ministry in holiness. The minister is not simply a "pious man" alongside of his ministerial duties, but he is essentially an "ecclesiastic," a man of and for the Church, preaching and living the Word of God in holiness so that he may efficaciously actualize the Church by and through his ministry *in persona Christi.*

It is also for this reason that we can say that Orders confer an "indelible character" on the one who is accepted into the ministry. This must not be understood in any physical or metaphysical way; nor is it "eternal" since all of the sacraments are signs signifying the living reality of God but in faith, in the shadows of time and will be temporary "until he comes" and we see God without veils of signs. The priestly character simply means that ordination, in the words of St. Thomas, places the ordained "in the face of the community in the name of Christ." The character of the priesthood is the visible rite of ordination by which the Church accepts one of the baptized for certain functions for the service of the rest of the community. He is thereby set apart but not separated

from men for certain functions as service to the
Church (prayer, the Eucharist, preaching, etc.).
It is evident that given this meaning of character,
future developments such as part time or temporary ministry are possible and probable. There
seems to be no dogmatic or theological reason why,
if pastoral reasons so warrant it, women as well as
men cannot be ordained for this sacrament function of ministry.

READINGS

1. J. P. Audet, *Structures of Christian Priesthood*
   (New York, 1965).
2. R. J. Bunnik, *Priests for Tomorrow* (New York,
   1969).
3. J. Fichter, *Religion as an Occupation* (Notre Dame,
   1961).
4. J. L. McKenzie, *Authority in the Church* (New
   York, 1966).
5. D. P. O'Neil, *Priestly Celibacy and Maturity* (New
   York, 1965).
6. M. Oraison, *The Celibate Condition and Sex* (New
   York, 1967).

DISCUSSION QUESTIONS

1. What is the sign and symbol of the sacrament of
   Orders?
2. What relationship is there between the sacrament
   of Orders and the Church?

3. Is it true that there is but one priest in Christianity? Explain.

4. How can there be more than one apostolate?

5. What does the priest symbolize at the celebration of the Eucharist?

6. What is the difference between the priesthood of the faithful and that of ordained ministers?

7. Can all of the priests of the world be without holiness at any one time? Why is holiness essential to the priesthood?

8. Compare the concept of the priesthood of the Council of Trent and that of Vatican II.

9. What is the relationship between the visibility of the Church and the visibility of the priesthood?

10. What is the essential function of the ordained ministry?

CHAPTER IX

Anointing of the Sick

There is much pastoral work and education to be done regarding this sacrament. The specific reference of this sacrament is the special spiritual comfort and experience of God's mercy at a critical moment of human existence, namely, when there is danger of death. In this sacrament, the Church stands by the seriously sick person (not necessarily the dying person) to comfort and bear witness to the eschatological hope of Christian existence which is implied in all of the sacraments but which meets the baptized in a particular way in this sacrament at this critical moment of the sick person when he needs the comfort of this hope in a very special way.

This sacrament—even among the faithful—is not a very popular one since it is usually administered when a person is actually dying or is already dead. This is bad pastoral practice and worse theology. In the early Church, this sacrament was never administered to the dying. For this, the Church gave *viatecum,* that is, the food of eternal life (Christ) to be with this dying man on the way to heaven. Moreover, it also betokens a pagan vision where death is the last word of human existence.

Essentially, the Church would not be church if it abandoned any of the faithful in one of their most trying moments since the Church is a pilgrim on earth with no abiding city here below; she is then, in the words of Vatican II, essentially related to the future who is God since God is the future and the hope of every man. In the words of St. Augustine: "Our hearts are restless, until they rest in thee." Consequently, every sacrament is related to this absolute future of man but since the sacraments are efficacious symbols of divine reality and hope for and in our human existence, then what more natural and indeed essential function of the Church could there be than a special sacrament which efficaciously symbolizes the future hope of the baptized so as thereby to strengthen him in his great hour of need? The Church calls this the sacramental reality and symbol of the anointing of the sick.

Vatican II explicitly taught that the Church is essentially eschatological in nature, that is, she is related absolutely to the future who is God (*Constitution on the Church,* par. 48–52). Yet, as we have also seen, it is we who are the Church in a true sense since the Church is made manifest and visible in history through her members who exist in this space and at this time. The Church is therefore the community of those who await in prayerful hope for the full manifestation of the Kingdom of God in the *Parousia* of Christ. She is essentially characterized by her longing for the last day when "there will be neither tear nor groan, but Christ in all." The Church's function in time is to await the bridegroom when he comes and to be prepared to meet him with shining lamps (i.e. good works) when he does come. It is in this faith and hope, living it out in active love, that each of the baptized await with longing this glorious expectation. It is not without reason that the New Testament concludes with the impatient cry: "Surely I am coming soon. Amen. Come, Lord Jesus!" (Rv 22:20).

For each of the faithful, the time of death (or its danger), is the supreme test of his faith in God, when he prepares to enter the definity of eternity. It is also at this moment that the world and all that is in it (wealth, power, prestige, etc.) are utterly powerless to give anyone meaning and hope and that is why the "world" retreats from death in embarrassed silence because it has nothing to offer man. The absolute insecurity of man's existence is clearly manifest at this supreme moment.

Not so the Church who comes to the seriously

sick man (who can really die) with the Word of the living God, that death is not a death to darkness (as was the death of Adam) but now his death in Christ (in which the baptized participated by his own baptism) is the entrance to eternal life (as in the death of Christ). That is why the early Church saw the anointing of the sick as the culmination of the sacraments of baptism and penance.

The whole Church stands by the sick man with the efficacious symbol of anointing and God's Word, to spiritually strengthen this sick man in hope and faith at a crucial moment of human existence. The whole Church stands by the sick man in this hope of eternal life in the form of the minister as well as those gathered around the sick bed: "Is any among you sick? Let him call for the elders of the Church, and let them pray over him, anointing him with oil in the name of the Lord; and the prayer of faith will save the sick man and the Lord will raise him up; and if he has committed sins, he will be forgiven" (Jas 5:14).

This symbol of anointing is not empty since it renders present what it proclaims (that is, the eschatological hope of every Christian in God, the absolute and loving future of man) and gives hope that even in the midst of the calamity and tragedy of sickness and possibly death, the signification of his death has been radically changed by and in the death of Christ. This sacrament gives the spiritual strength to the sick man to be fortified in the fact that the image of death (which, humanly, seems to be utter ruin and a return to the nothingness from which we came), has now been changed by and in the death of Christ in which the baptized has been incorporated and saved. The anointing of the sick gives and strengthens the hope and faith of the sick man in making this reality of salvation his own during this most critical moment of his human existence. Death does not and cannot have the final say since God has responded to our fear and despair of death, in the eschatological promise of himself, who is love, for all eternity.

It is true that this sacrament is not simply a preparation for death (for this the Church has reserved the *viatecum,* the Eucharist, which is in the words of the ancients, the "medicine of immortality") but is more broadly related to any sickness which might result in the final terminal point of human existence in which we seal our fate forever (death). It is also true that often this sacrament so spiritually strengthens and consoles the person that it actually has an effect for the better on the body of the sick person (since man is a total entity of both body and soul, if we wish to speak in this way).

It is for this reason that many theologians have said (and the Church itself) that the secondary effect of the anointing of the sick is bodily health. This is true if we keep in mind what we have said concerning the hope and faith in the eschatological word of God strengthened specifically by this sacrament. If bodily health also ensues, this is good but then there will always be *a* sickness which will end in death. God's saving grace and love is total in that it saves man totally, in body and in soul. The doctrine of the resurrection is an integral part of the Christian reality so that whether the anointing of the sick has its effect (indirectly) on the bodily health now of the sick person or prepares and strengthens his faith in the ultimate resurrection, is, of course, only in the merciful hands of God. In either case, the Christian reality of eschatological hope remains essential to the sacrament. The anointing of the sick cannot do away with this inherent ambiguity of sickness but it always leads (in the willing and receptive faithful) to a supernatural victory over sickness.

This victory consists in overcoming the hindrances to God's love, mercy and grace within us, adding spiritual strength to the sick person's spiritual life by increasing his faith and trust as well as forgiveness of sins to him who is rightly disposed. For the greatest victory over sickness is a Christian death. According to the disposition of the recipient this grace and his cooperation with it, does he prepare himself for the final hope of entrance into the fullness of God's unveiled glory.

READINGS

1. L. Boros, *The Mystery of Death* (New York, 1965).
2. I. Lepp, *Death and its Mysteries* (New York, 1968).

3. M. Oraison, *Death and Then What?* (Westminster, Md., 1969).

4. P. F. Palmer, *Sources of Christian Theology*. II. *Sacraments and Forgiveness* (Westminster, Md., 1960).

5. B. Poschmann, *Penance and the Anointing of the Sick* (New York, 1964).

6. K. Rahner, *On the Theology of Death* (New York, 1964).

DISCUSSION QUESTIONS

1. What is the sign and symbol of the sacrament of the sick?

2. What is the relationship between the sacrament of the sick and the Church?

3. Why do we call this sacrament, the sacrament of the *sick*?

4. When should this sacrament be administered?

5. What is the Christian meaning of death?

6. What do we mean when we say that God is man's absolute future?

7. Why are all created things incapable of giving man a meaning to his existence?

8. How can the whole Church stand by the sick man in his hour of need?

9. In what way is bodily recovery a secondary effect of this sacrament?